BEGIN … TORY

TUDOR SAILORS

Roger Coote

Illustrated by John James

Wayland

BEGINNING HISTORY

The Age of Exploration
The American West
Crusaders
Egyptian Farmers
Egyptian Pyramids
Family Life in World War II
Greek Cities
The Gunpowder Plot
Medieval Markets
Norman Castles
Plague and Fire
Roman Cities
Roman Soldiers
Saxon Villages
Tudor Sailors
Tudor Towns
Victorian Children
Victorian Factory Workers
Viking Explorers
Viking Warriors

All words that appear in **bold** are explained in the glossary on page 22.

Series editor: Catherine Ellis
Designer: Helen White

First published in 1989 by Wayland (Publishers) Limited,
61 Western Road, Hove, East Sussex BN3 1JD

British Library Cataloguing in Publication Data
Coote, Roger
Tudor Sailors
1. English ships. Sailors. Social conditions, history
I. Title II. Series
305.9'3875

HARDBACK ISBN 1-85210-815-0

PAPERBACK ISBN 0-7502-0891-0

Typeset by Kalligraphic Design Limited, Horley, Surrey.
Printed in Italy by G. Canale & C.S.p.A., Turin.
Bound in Belgium by Casterman S.A.

CONTENTS

EXPLORATION AND TRADE

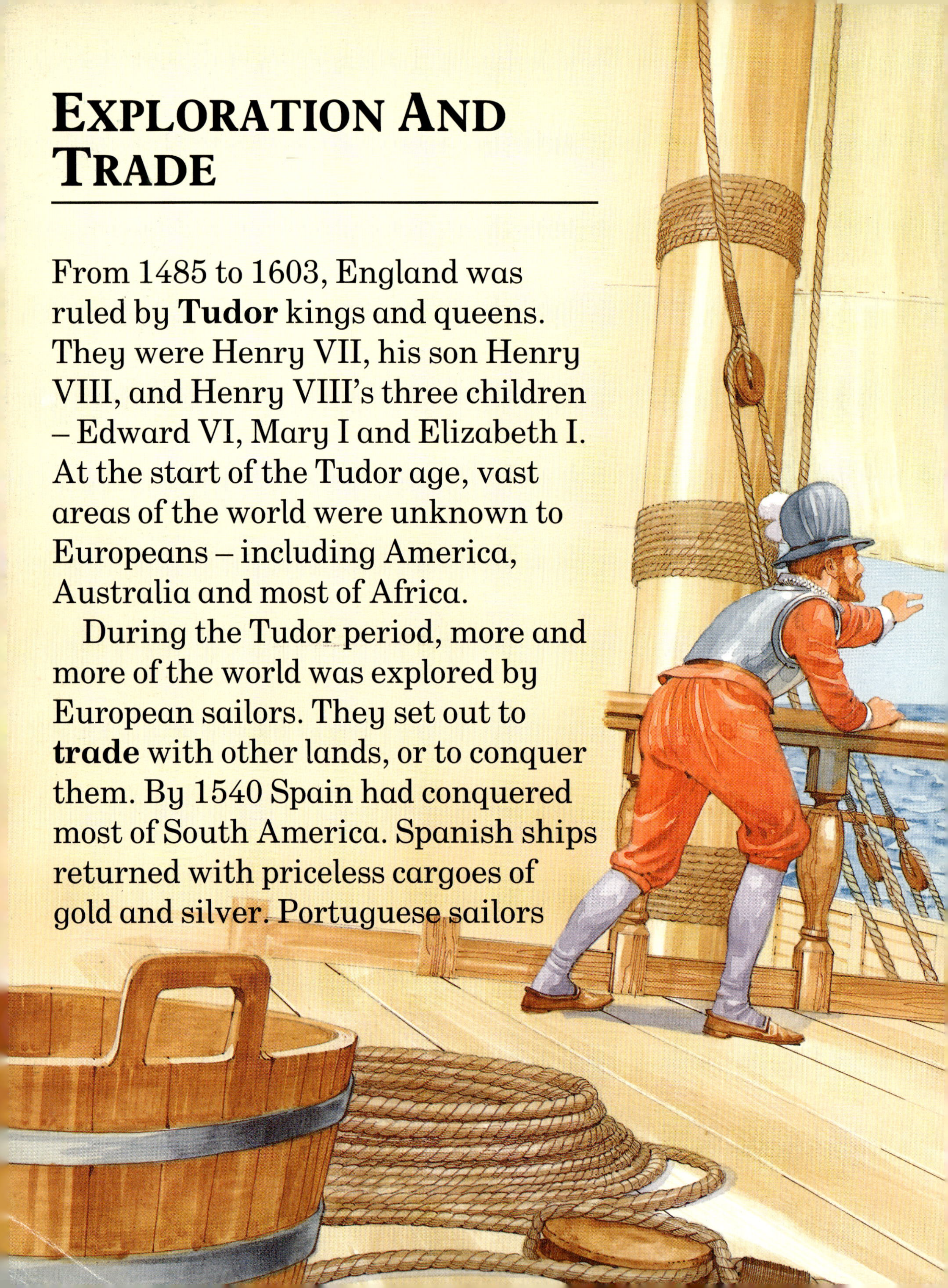

From 1485 to 1603, England was ruled by **Tudor** kings and queens. They were Henry VII, his son Henry VIII, and Henry VIII's three children – Edward VI, Mary I and Elizabeth I. At the start of the Tudor age, vast areas of the world were unknown to Europeans – including America, Australia and most of Africa.

During the Tudor period, more and more of the world was explored by European sailors. They set out to **trade** with other lands, or to conquer them. By 1540 Spain had conquered most of South America. Spanish ships returned with priceless cargoes of gold and silver. Portuguese sailors had found a route to the **Spice Islands** in the Far East, around the southern tip of Africa. Their ships brought back valuable **spices**, silk and gold.

English **merchants** also began to look beyond Europe. They wanted some of the rich Spanish and Portuguese trade for themselves.

In Tudor times, sailors from Europe visited lands which were previously unknown.

A reconstruction of Drake's ship The Golden Hind.

Below *Utensils from the wreck of the* Mary Rose.

A SAILOR'S LIFE

In Tudor times, merchant ships were made of wood. They had three masts with canvas sails. Most ships carried a few cannon, to fight off attacking **pirates**. Above the main deck, at the **bow** and the **stern**, were smaller raised decks, called 'castles'. They contained the Captain's cabin and other cabins for the officers.

Life was hard for the ordinary seamen. They had to sleep on the

deck, wherever they could find a space. They were usually wet and cold, with no fires to warm them. Their food was stored in the **hold** below the decks, along with the cargo. This was the dirtiest part of the ship. It was infested with rats and mice.

On long voyages meat often went rotten, the **ship's biscuit** became full of worms, and the drinking water turned green. There was no fresh food. Many sailors died of diseases due to poor diet, or food poisoning.

A cut-away view of a large Tudor merchant ship. The small inset picture shows the ship in full sail.

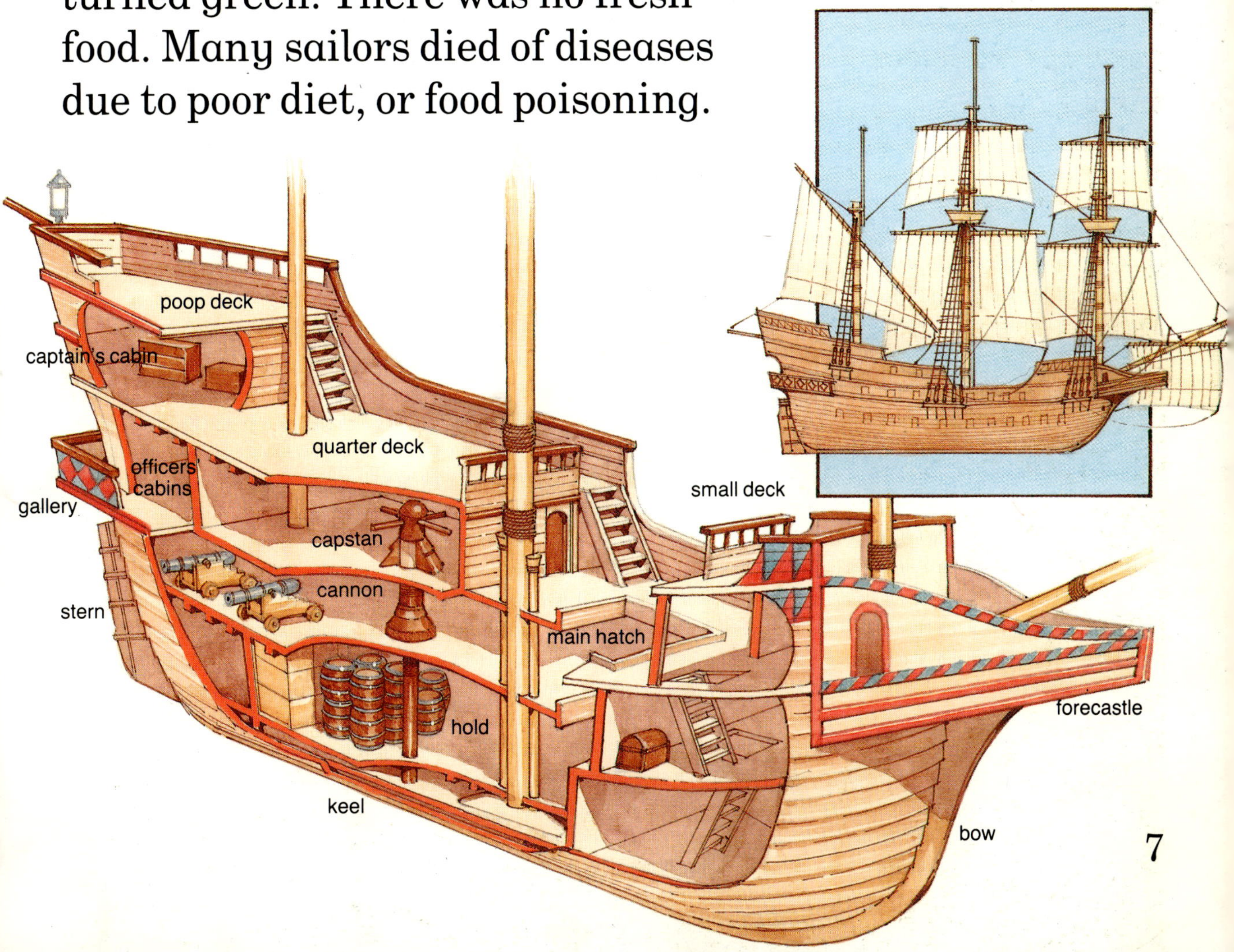

The Cabots twice sailed north-west across the Atlantic in search of a route to China.

THE FIRST ADVENTURERS

In 1497, John Cabot set sail from Bristol with his son Sebastian. They headed across the Atlantic, hoping to find a way to China. The Cabots first reached Nova Scotia in Canada. They then sailed north to Newfoundland. When he returned to England, John Cabot claimed that he had reached the East. King Henry VII was very pleased, and agreed to give him money for another voyage.

John and Sebastian Cabot prepare to leave Bristol on their first voyage in 1497.

So Cabot set out again in 1498. He sailed north-west to Greenland, and then southward down the coast of Canada. He may have sailed as far as Delaware Bay, more than half-way down the North American coast. On his return journey, Cabot's ship was lost and he never returned home.

Eleven years later, his son Sebastian again tried to find a route to Asia. He sailed into Canada's Hudson Bay but could get no further, so he returned home.

HAWKINS AND THE SLAVE TRADE

The first English seaman to sail to South America was John Hawkins. He went to trade with the settlers in Spain's **colonies** there. In 1562 he set out with three ships to West Africa. There he took on board 300 Africans. Some of them were **slaves** bought with beads and knives. Others he took by force. He then sailed across to South America and sold the Africans as slaves to the Spanish settlers. He returned to England with silver, pearls and animal skins. Two years

Hawkins and his men loading slaves in West Africa.

later he made another successful voyage. But disaster struck on the third journey, in 1567.

Spain wanted to keep the South American trade to itself. When Hawkins and his men reached San Juan de Ulua, in Mexico, they were attacked by a Spanish fleet. Many English seamen died. Hawkins managed to escape, along with a young sailor called Francis Drake. Drake vowed revenge against the Spanish for their treachery.

PIRATES AND PRIVATEERS

Trading ships were often attacked by well-armed **pirates** and **privateers** who stole their cargo. Spanish and Portuguese ships were frequent victims because of their valuable cargoes. English privateers sailed down the coasts of Spain and Portugal searching for treasure ships to attack and **plunder**.

After the Spanish attack at San Juan de Ulua, English pirates and privateers began seizing Spanish ships in the Caribbean. Among them was a man called John Oxenham. In 1577, Oxenham captured two ships carrying cargoes of silver. He was caught and hanged by the Spaniards.

The most feared privateer of all was Francis Drake. He attacked many treasure ships and even a Spanish town in South America. In 1573 he ambushed a mule-train in Panama. He escaped with a hoard of Spanish silver and returned to England in triumph.

A Spanish treasure ship under attack by pirates in the Caribbean.

Queen Elizabeth I knights Sir Francis Drake after his round-the-world voyage.

AROUND THE WORLD

Drake's greatest voyage began in 1577. From Plymouth he sailed across the Atlantic and down the South American coast. He rounded Cape Horn and entered the Pacific Ocean. Sailing north, he raided Spanish treasure ships and settlements along the coasts of Chile

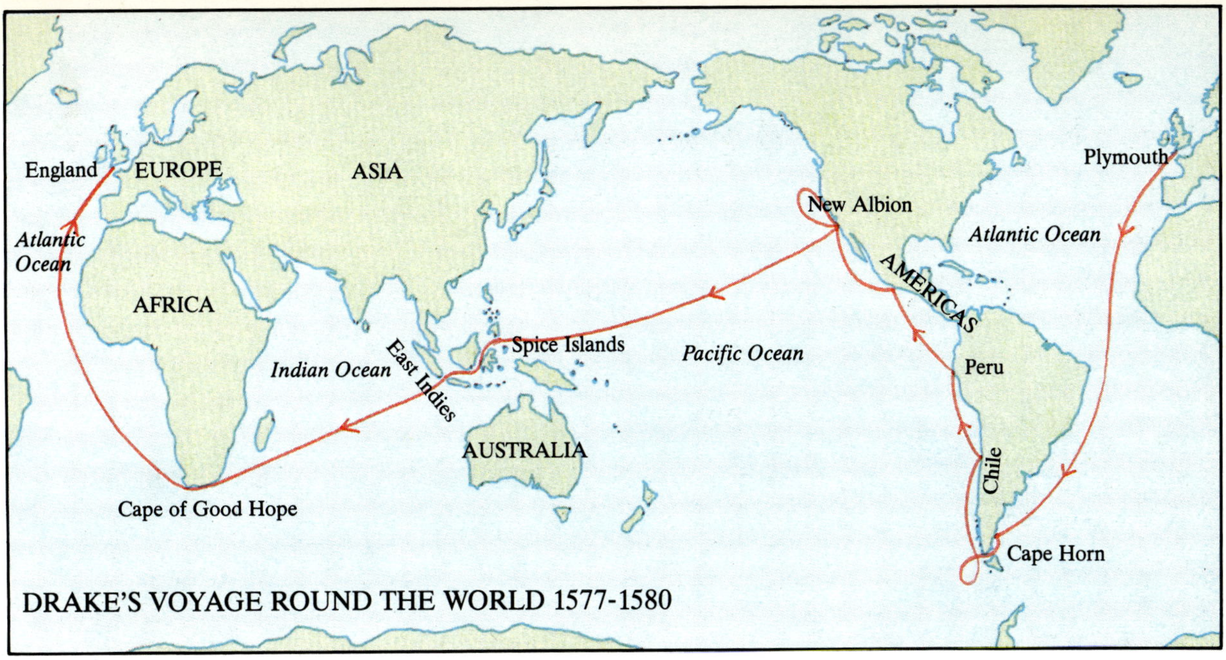

and Peru. Then he sailed on to what is now California. He named the land New Albion.

Turning west, Drake headed across the Pacific. He was welcomed by the **Sultan** of the Spice Islands, and the two men signed a treaty. After taking on board some valuable spices, Drake sailed for home. He reached Plymouth in October 1580. His round-the-world voyage had taken almost three years. The treasure he had captured was worth a fortune – for himself and for Queen Elizabeth. She was delighted by Drake's success. In 1581 she knighted him aboard his ship *The Golden Hind*.

Below *Sir Francis Drake (c. 1540–1596).*

English and Spanish ships fighting at close range.

THE SPANISH ARMADA

In 1585 Spain and England went to war. King Philip II of Spain decided to send a large fleet to invade England. But in 1587 Francis Drake launched a daring attack on Cadiz harbour in Spain. He destroyed or captured twenty-two Spanish ships. Philip had to delay the planned invasion.

In 1588, the 130 ships of the Spanish **Armada** finally set sail, arriving off Cornwall in July. They then headed for Dunkirk to pick up a large Spanish army. Lord Howard (the English commander), Drake and

John Hawkins followed.

On 7 August both fleets were anchored off Calais. Suddenly the Spaniards saw flames as English **fireships** drifted towards them. The Spanish fleet scattered in panic. English ships chased them and the two fleets fought fiercely. Then a storm blew the Armada northward. Many Spanish ships were wrecked as they tried to sail home around Scotland. The invasion had failed.

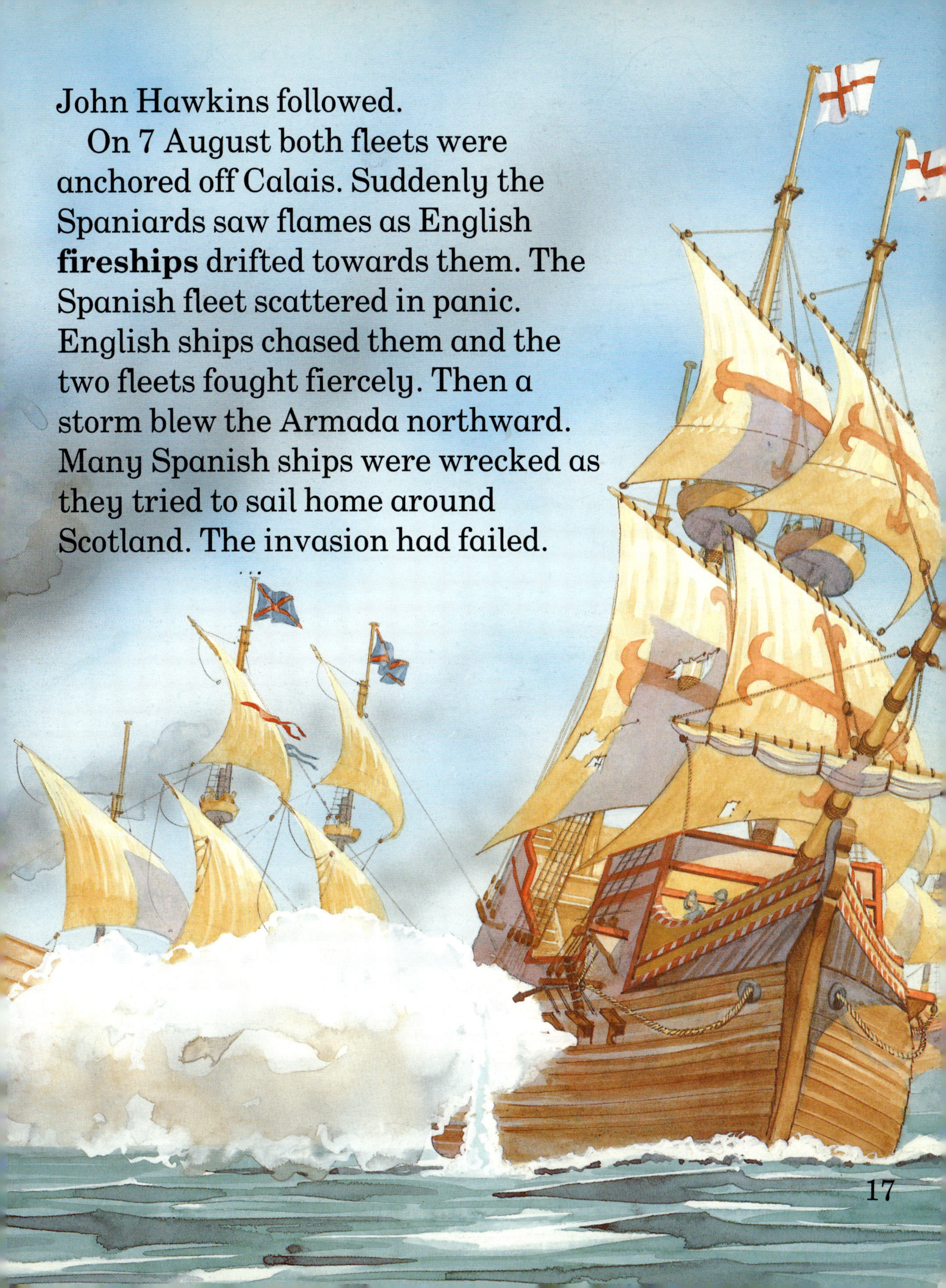

North-east and North-west

Tudor merchants were keen to trade with China, India and the Spice Islands. But it took a long time to sail around Africa or South America to reach the East. They wanted a shorter route.

Some sailors looked for a 'north-east passage' to the north of Russia. Sir Hugh Willoughby and Richard Chancellor tried in 1553, but failed.

Some people believed it was possible to reach the East by sailing around the north of Canada. The

Frobisher is attacked by Inuit hunters in Greenland.

Cabots had failed to discover this 'north-west passage', but merchants put up money for new expeditions. Between 1576 and 1578 Martin Frobisher made three voyages to Baffin Island, in the far north of Canada. Each time he was stopped by ice. John Davis also tried and failed about ten years later. Eventually, people realized that a north-west passage does not exist.

A Tudor captain and his officers examine the ship's charts.

RALEGH AND THE NEW WORLD

Tudor seamen attempted several times to start colonies in North America. Sir Humphrey Gilbert tried in Newfoundland in 1583, but he was unsuccessful. Two years later Sir Walter Ralegh sent settlers to a colony at Roanoke Island, in what we now call North Carolina. Life in the colony was very hard and the settlers returned home after a year.

Sir Walter Ralegh tried twice to set up colonies in North America.

Ralegh tried again in 1587. He sent another group of about one hundred settlers to begin a new colony. At that time England was at war with Spain. There were no English ships available to take supplies to the colony until 1591. When the first supply ship did arrive, the colony was deserted. The settlers had all mysteriously vanished. Only their empty huts remained. They may have been killed by local people.

Some successful colonies were set up later, after the Tudor period.

Above *English settlers arriving in North America.* **Below** *Tudor sailors used instruments like these to navigate across the oceans.*

GLOSSARY

Armada A Spanish word meaning 'fleet of ships'.

Bow The front of a ship.

Colony A place where a group of people from another country settle and live.

Fireships Ships filled with quick-burning materials, such as tar and straw. They were set on fire and left to float towards enemy ships.

Hold The part of a ship, below the deck, where the cargo is stored.

Merchant A person who buys goods and then sells them at a higher price.

Pirate A person who attacks ships at sea and steals the cargo for his own gain.

Plunder To steal valuable things by force.

Privateer A person who is given permission, by a monarch or other important person, to rob foreign ships.

Ship's biscuit Hard, biscuit-like food eaten by sailors. It was taken on sea voyages because it did not go rotten as quickly as fresh food.

Slave A person who is owned by someone else and has to do whatever he or she is told.

Spice A strong-tasting substance, such as pepper, used in cooking.

Spice Islands A group of islands in the Far East where many spices were grown. They are now known as the Moluccas.

Stern The back part of a ship.

Sultan A ruler of a country.

Trade Buying and selling goods or exchanging one sort of goods for another.

Tudor A member of the Tudor family. Also the name of the period when the Tudor family ruled England.

BOOKS TO READ

A Tudor Merchant by Barry and Anne Steel (Wayland, 1986).

The Tudors by Tim Pashley (Wayland, 1985).

Elizabeth I and Tudor England by S. White-Thomson (Wayland, 1984).

See Inside a Galleon by Jonathan Rutland (Kingfisher, 1988).

Drake and the Armada by Fiona Macdonald (Macdonald, 1988).

The Age of Drake by Leonard Cowie (Wayland, 1972).

Picture acknowledgements

The publishers would like to thank the following for providing the photographs in this book: The Mary Rose Trust 6 (bottom), 21 (bottom); Peter Newark's Historical Pictures 9, 10, 15 (bottom); Peter Newark's Western Americana 21 (top); Topham Picture Library 6 (top); Wayland Picture Library 18. The map on page 15 is by Malcolm Walker.

INDEX